Hand-Illustrated by Jules Baker

Letter Doodles

ALPHABET COLORING BOOK

This book is dedicated to my wonderful family. My husband Stephen, and my son Mikey. They mean the world to me.
And I can't forget my Kickstarter campaign backers, who invested and believed in my art. Without their financial support, I wouldn't have been able to complete my book.

Website: www.JulesBakerArtStudio.com

This Page Intentionally Left Blank

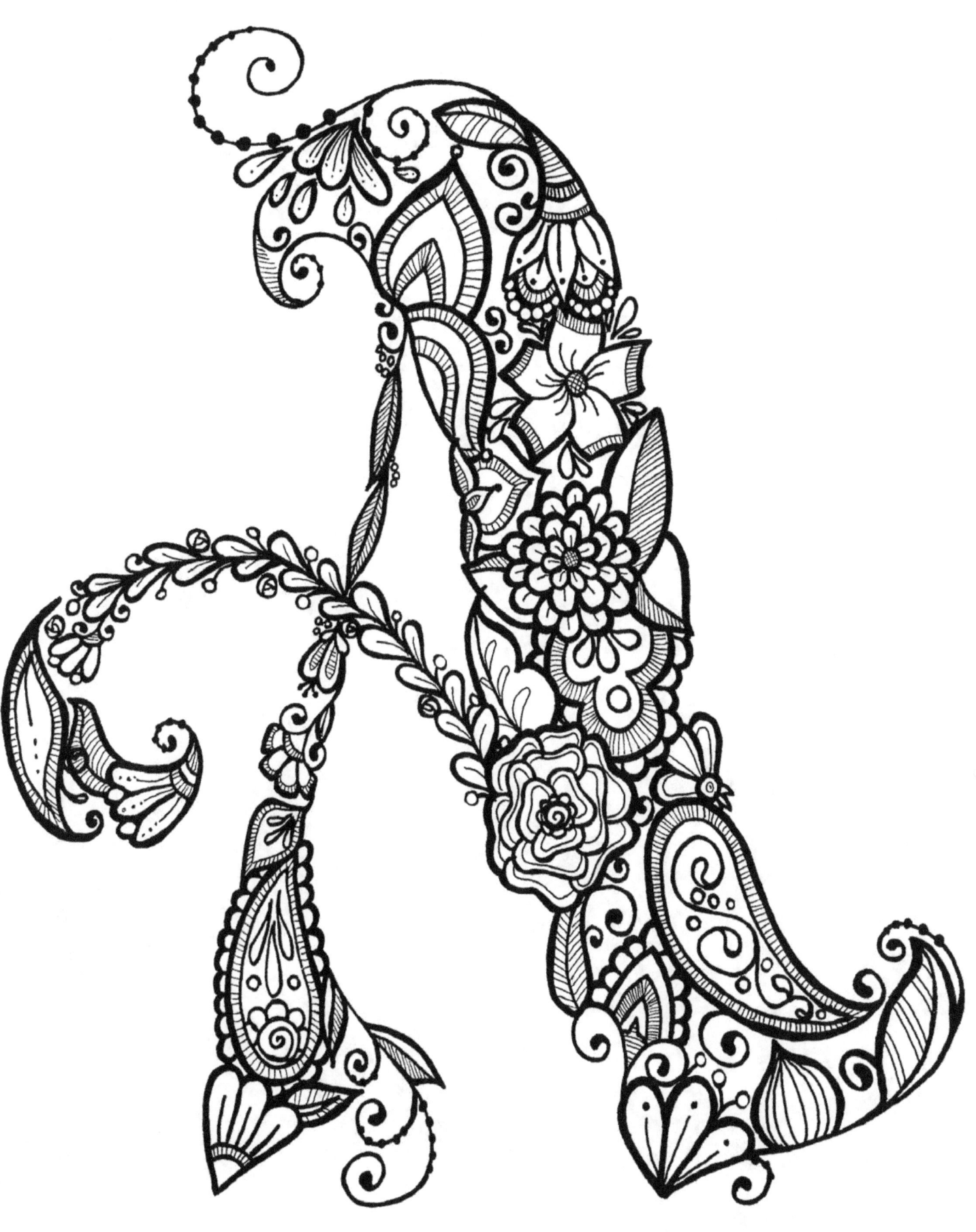

This Page Intentionally Left Blank

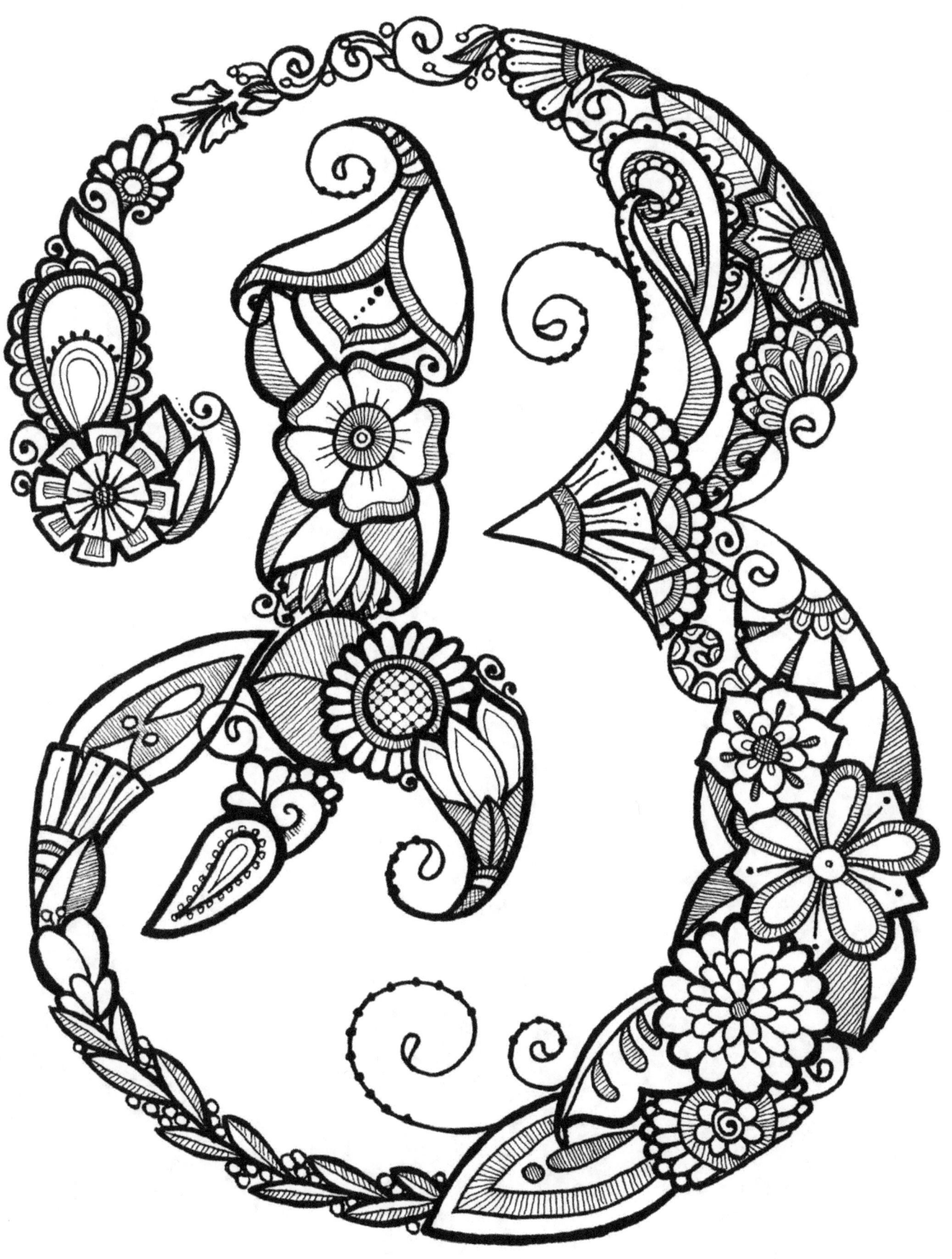

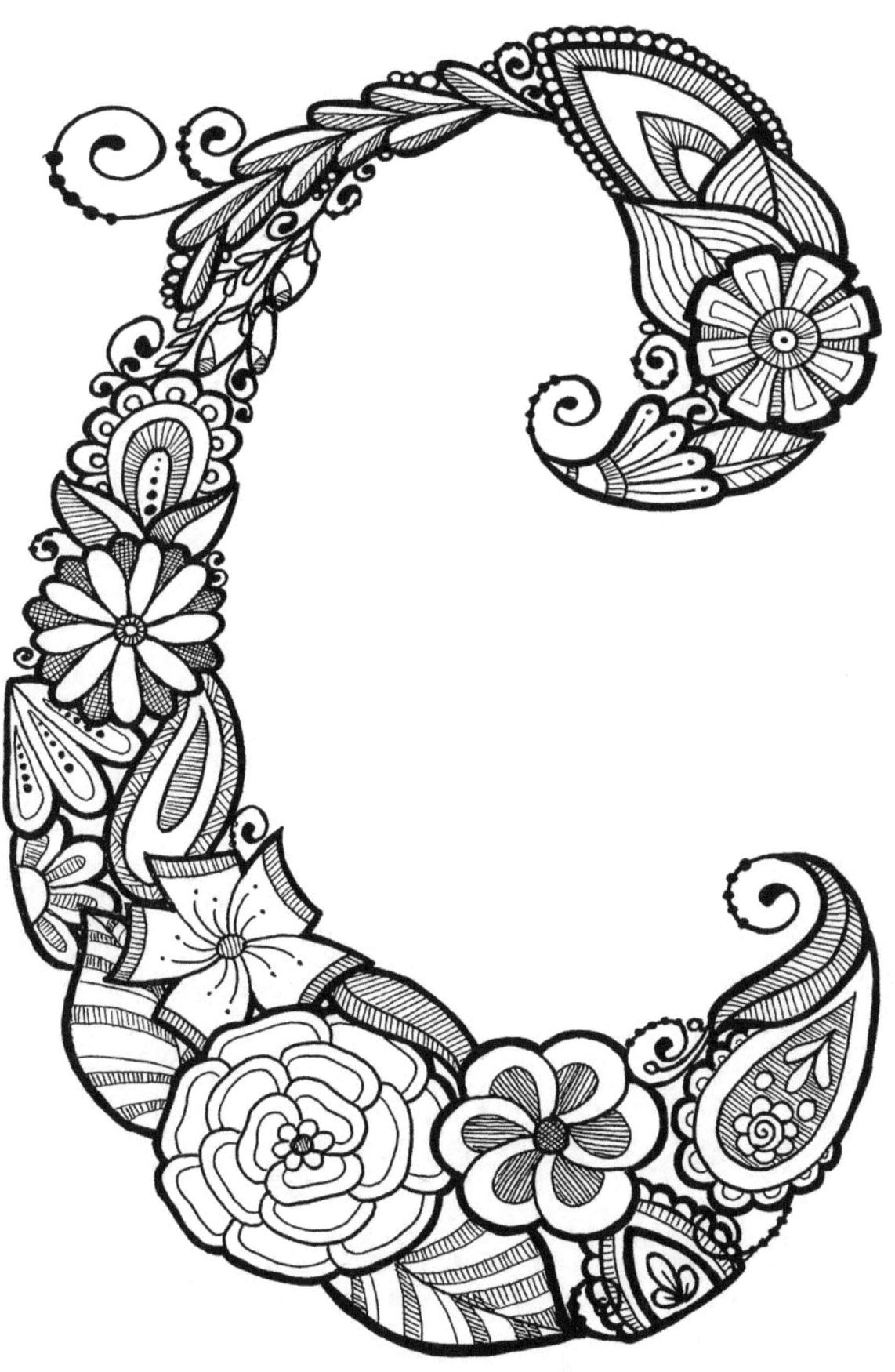

This Page Intentionally Left Blank

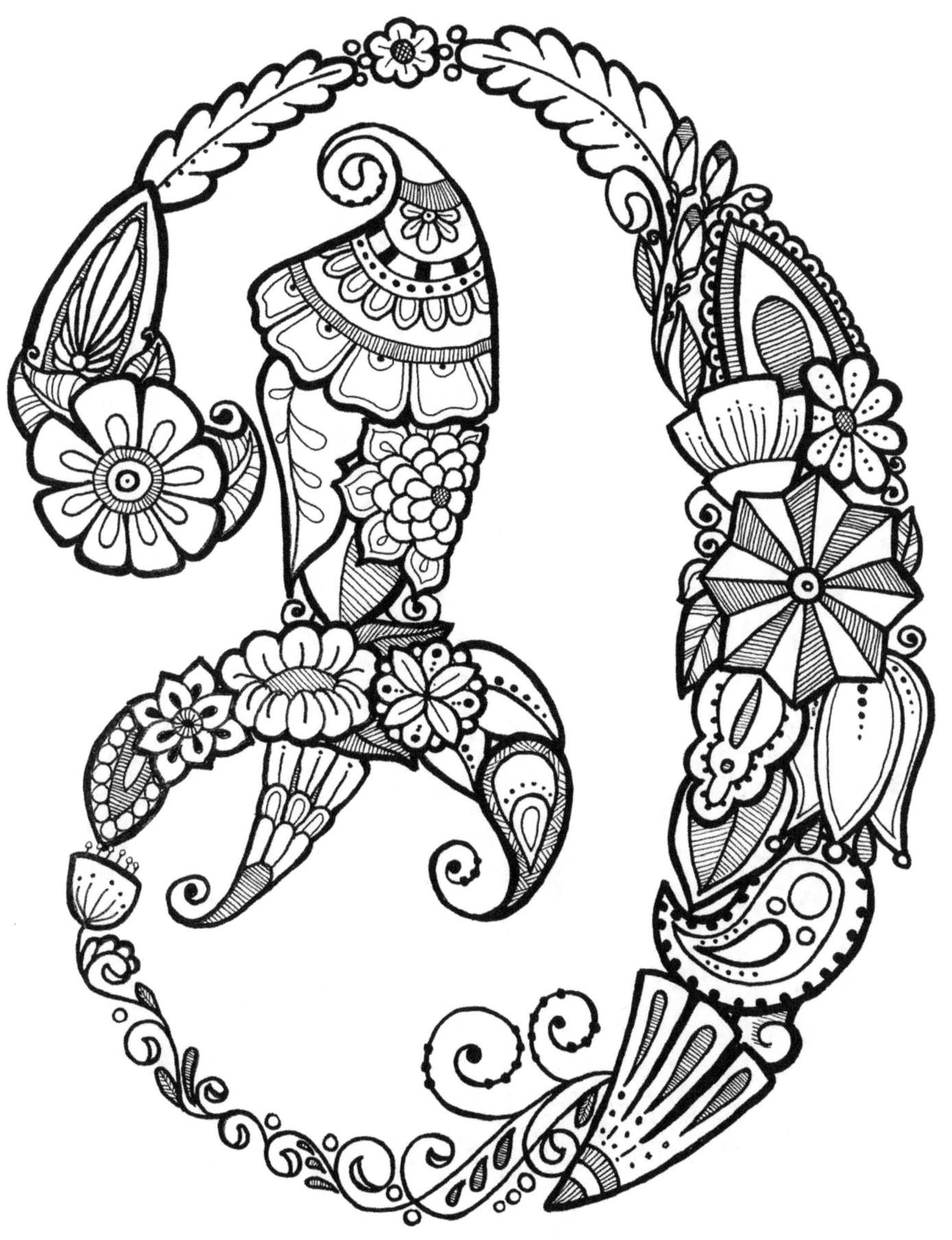

This Page Intentionally Left Blank

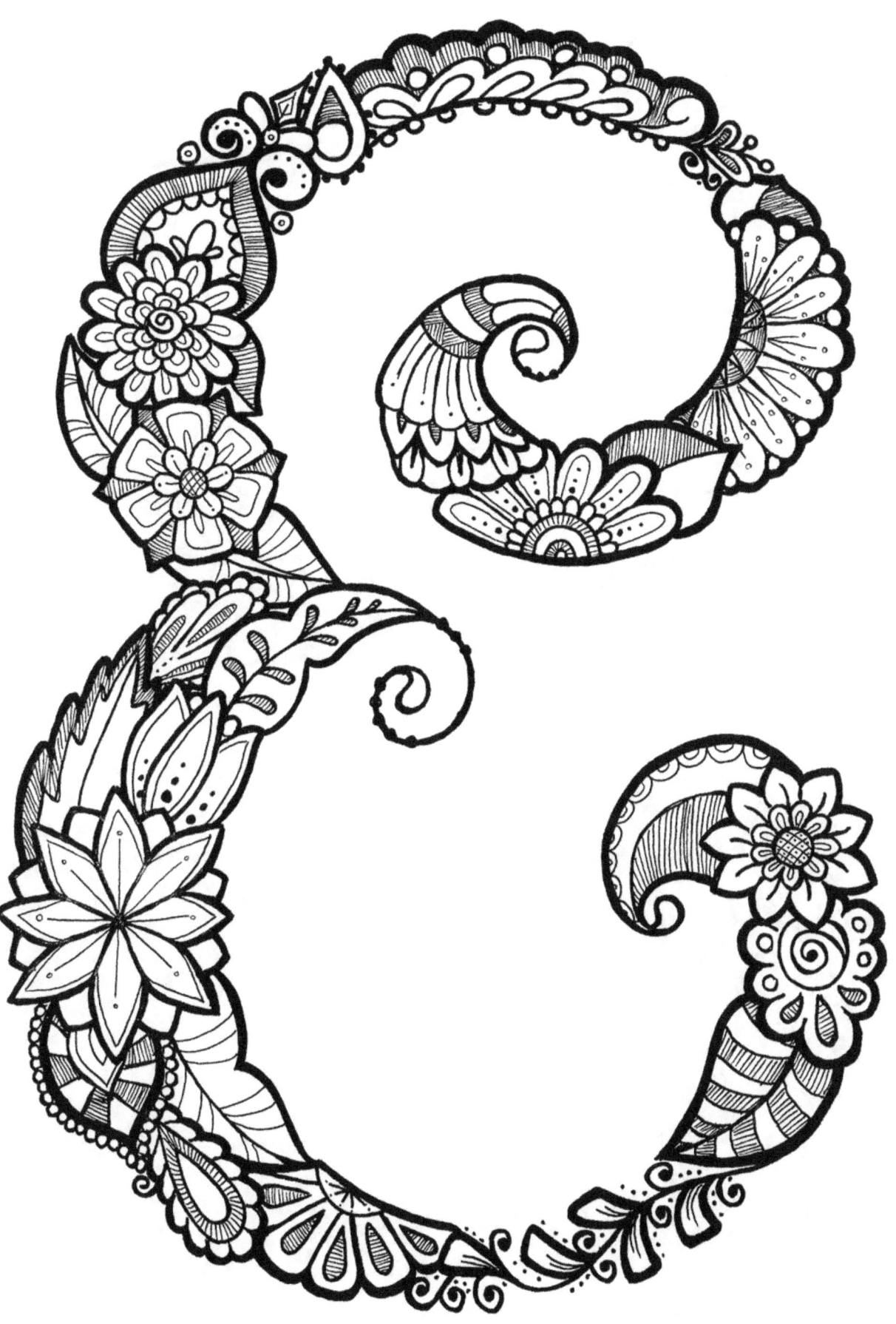

This Page Intentionally Left Blank

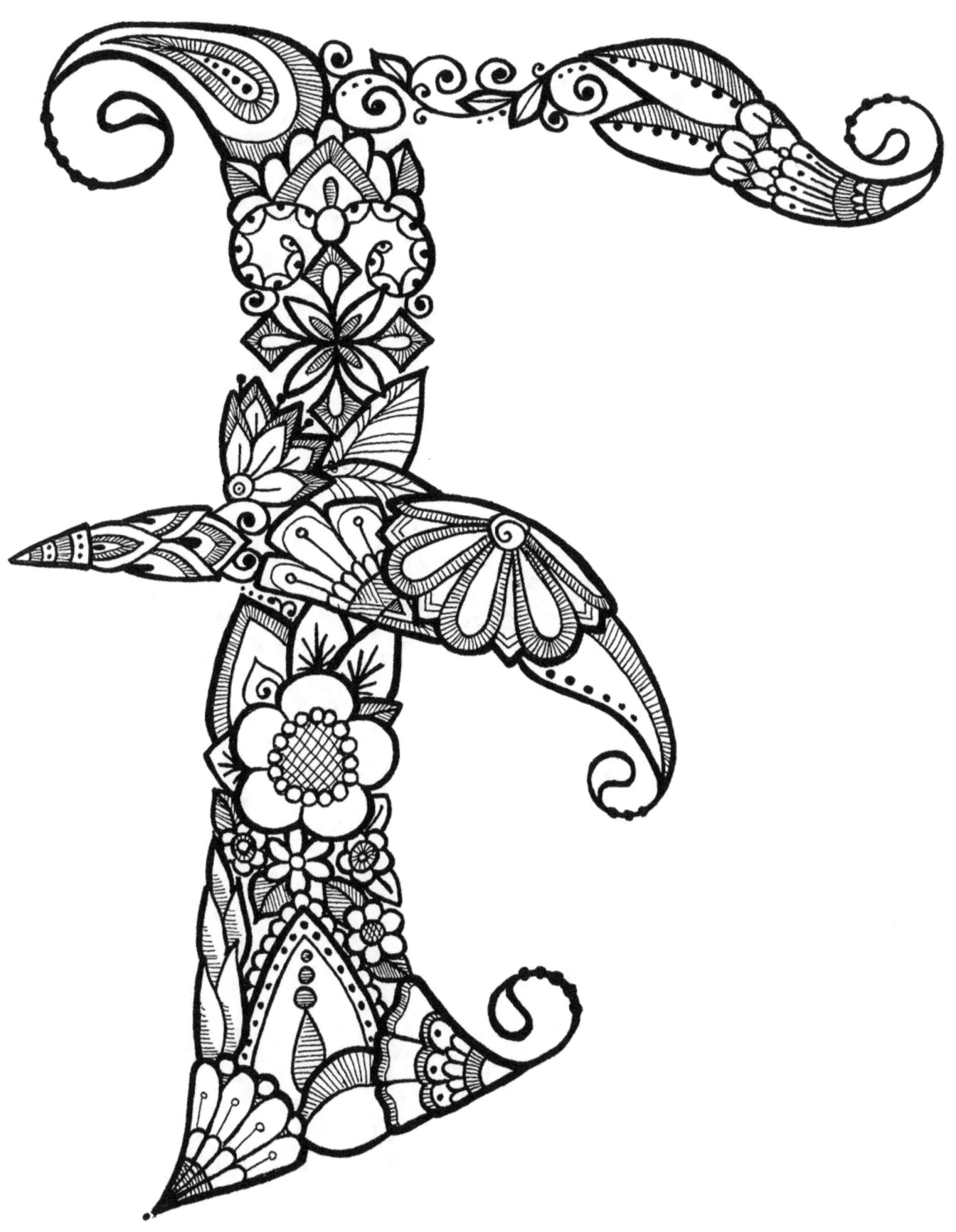

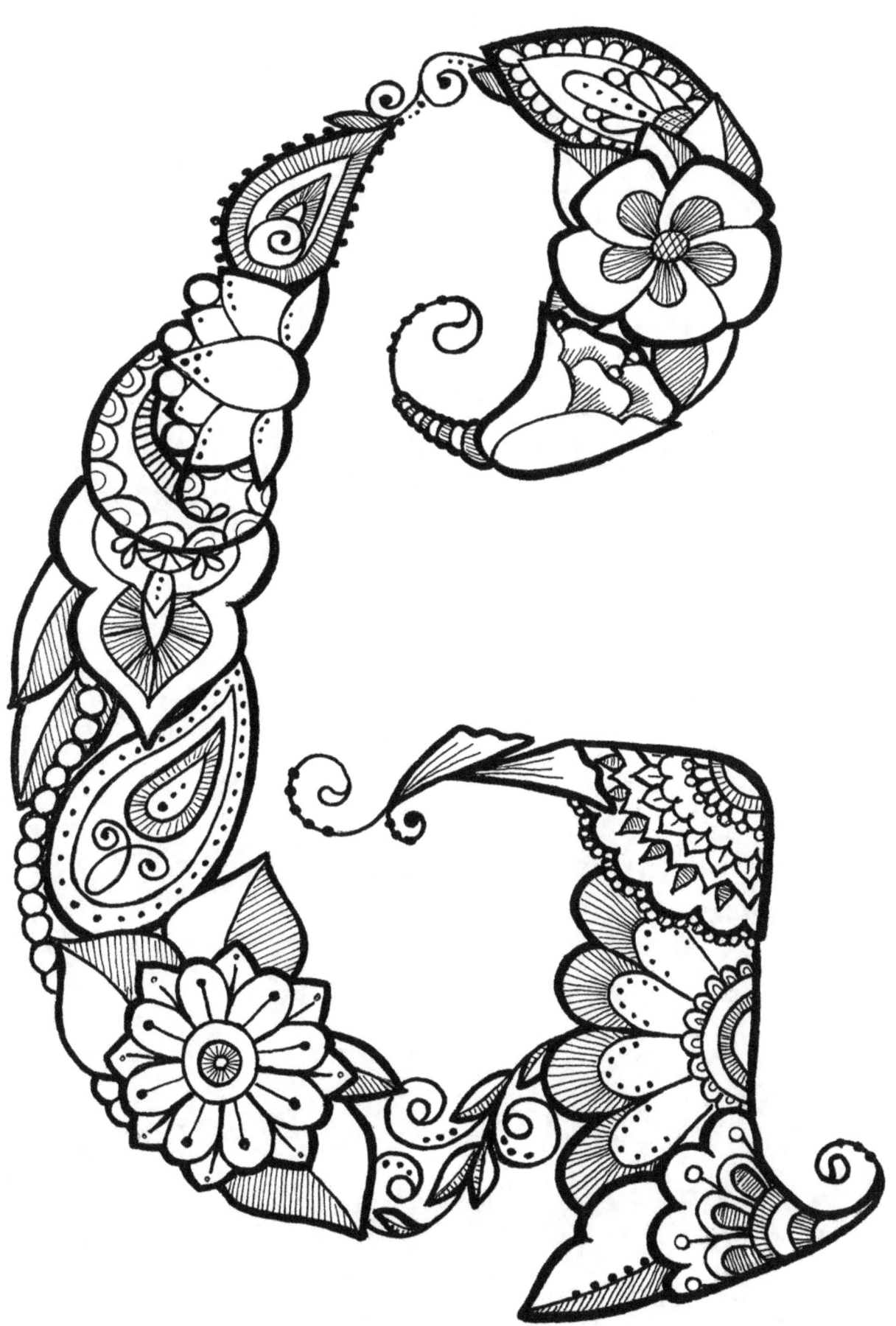

This Page Intentionally Left Blank

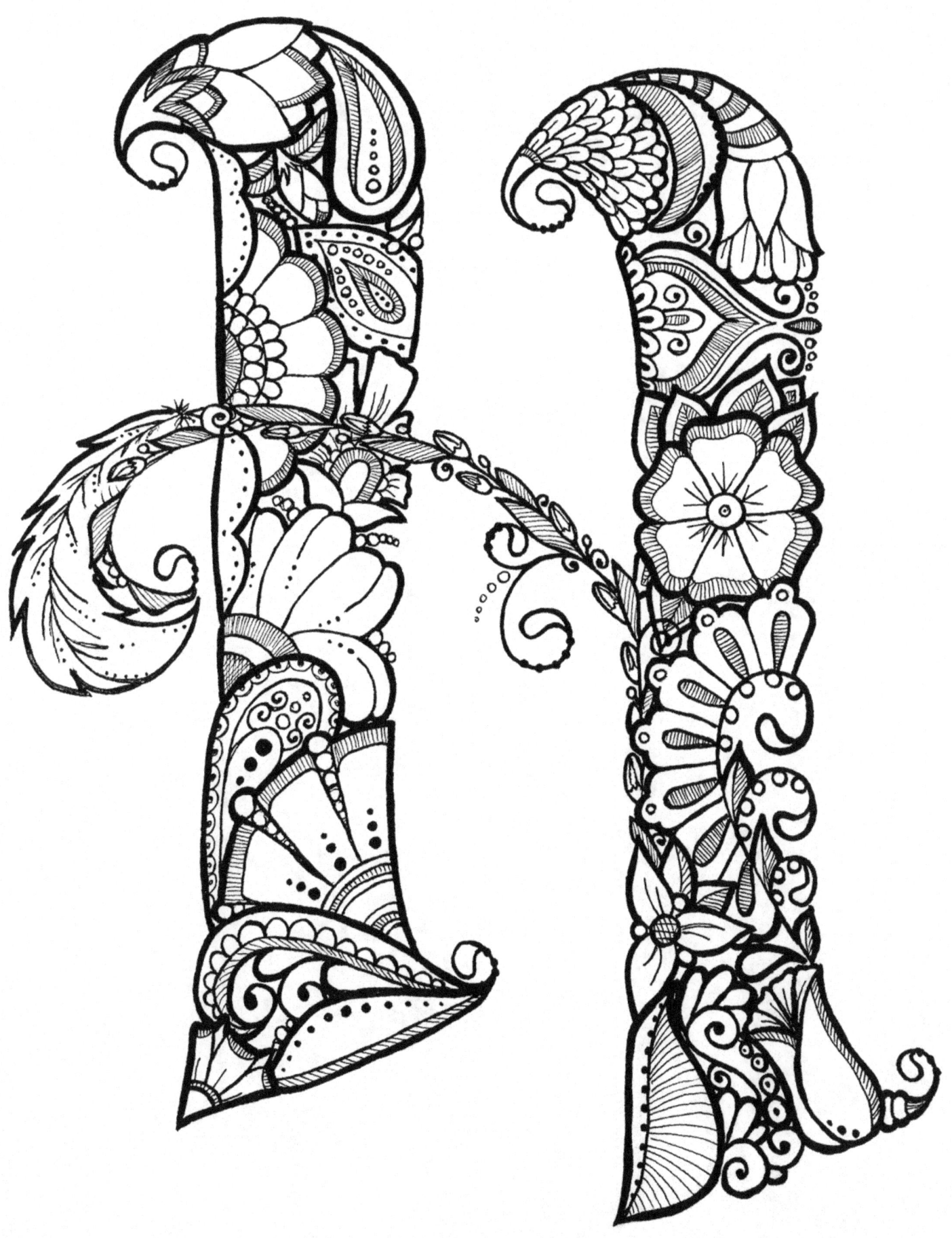

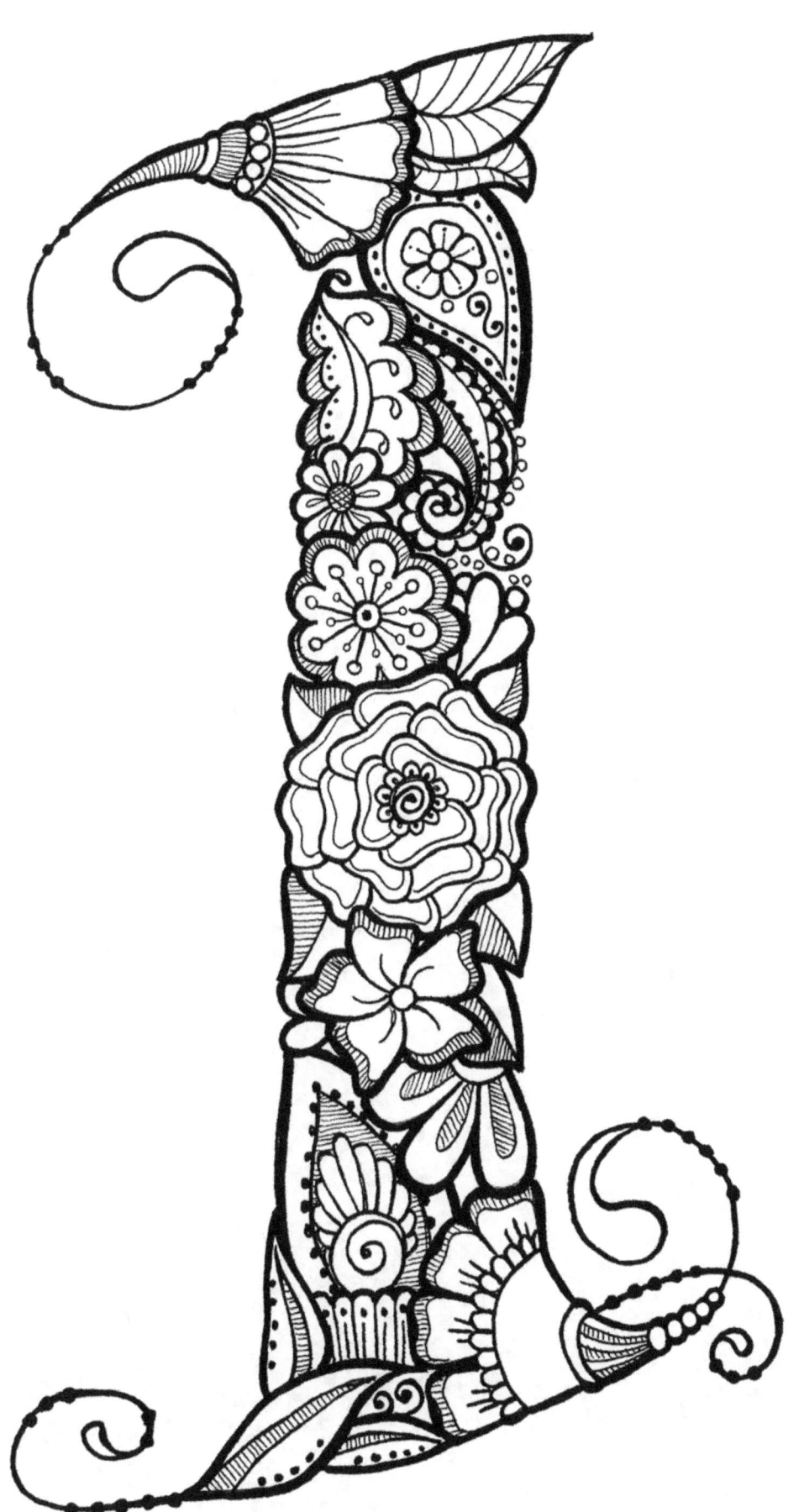

This Page Intentionally Left Blank

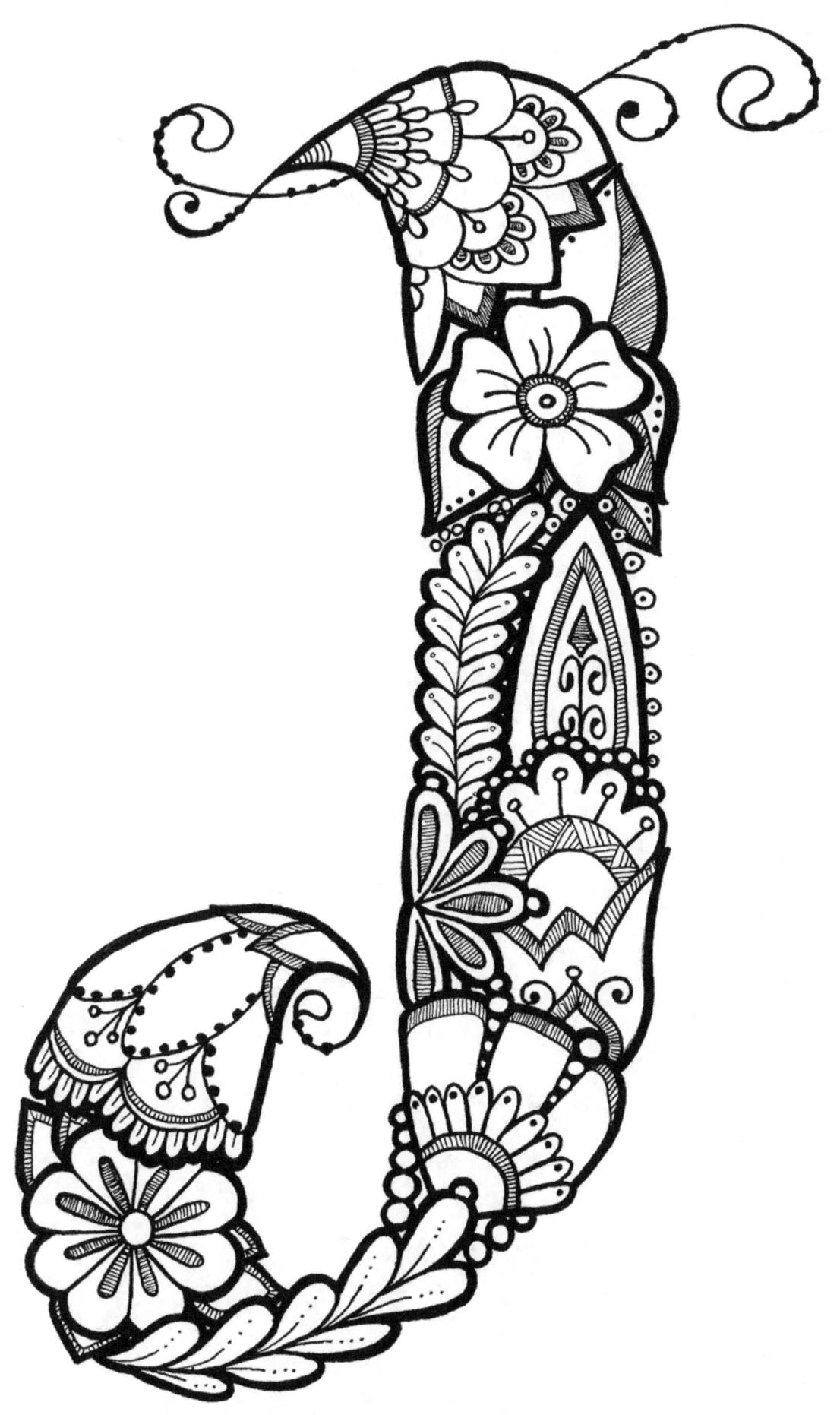

This Page Intentionally Left Blank

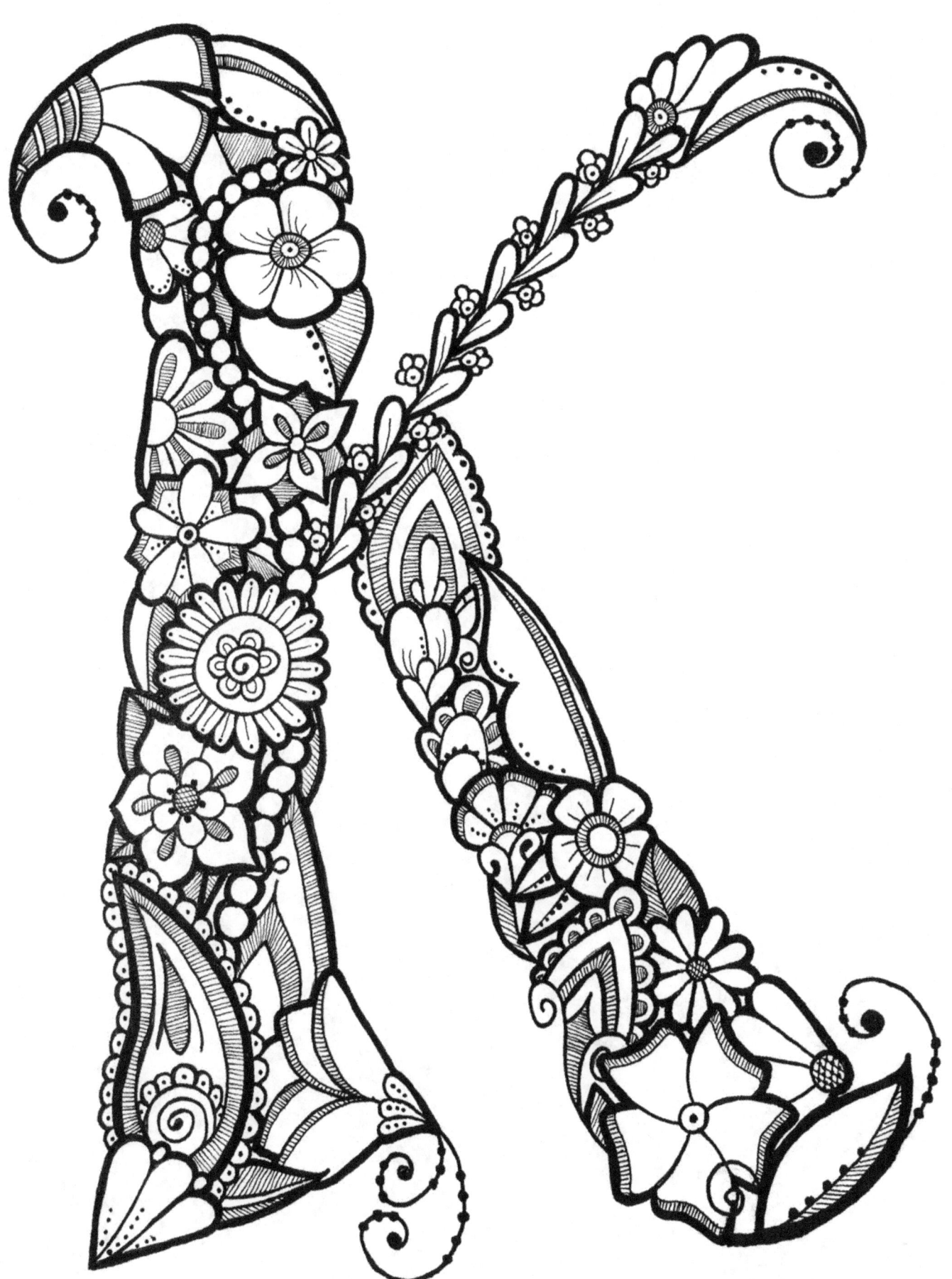

This Page Intentionally Left Blank

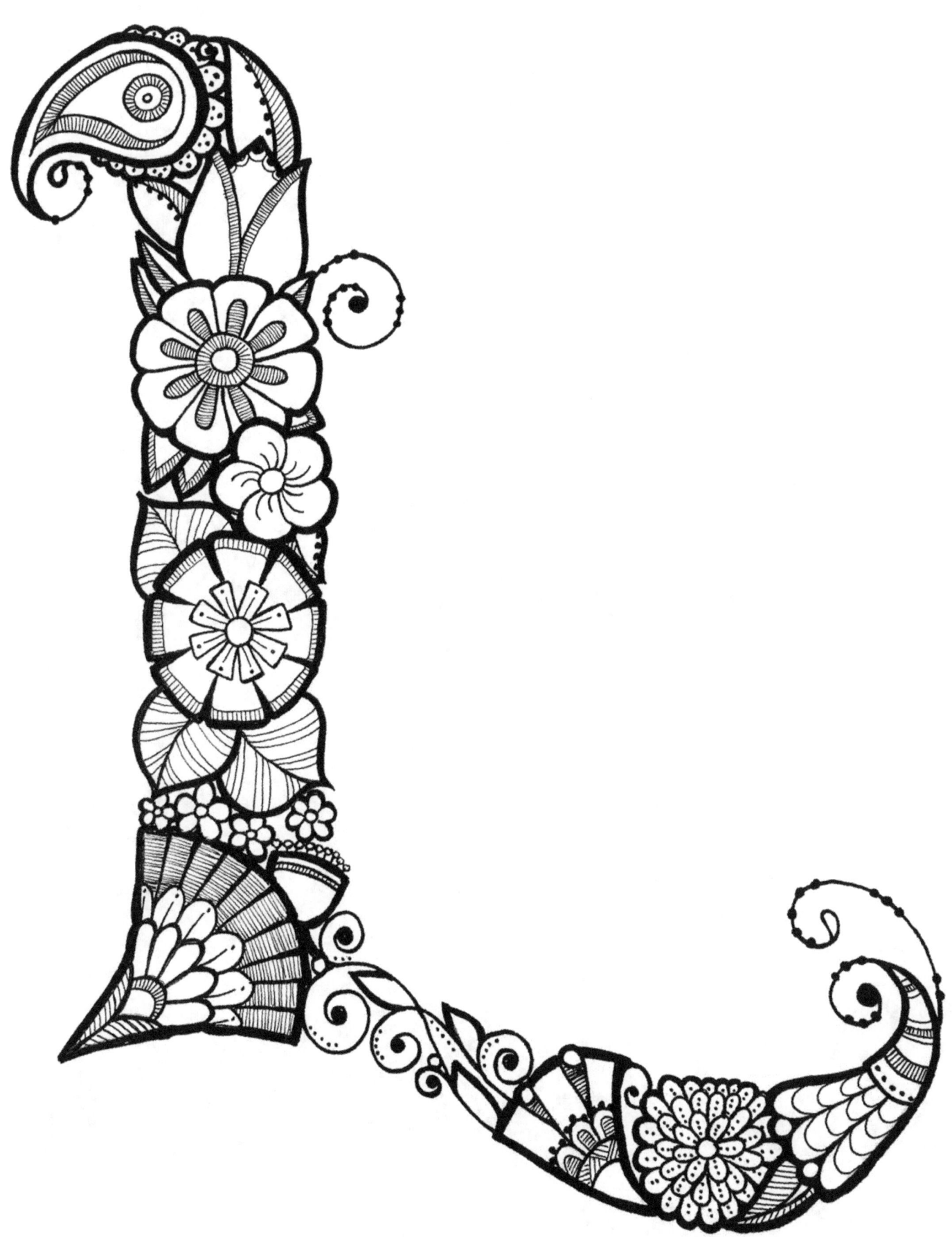

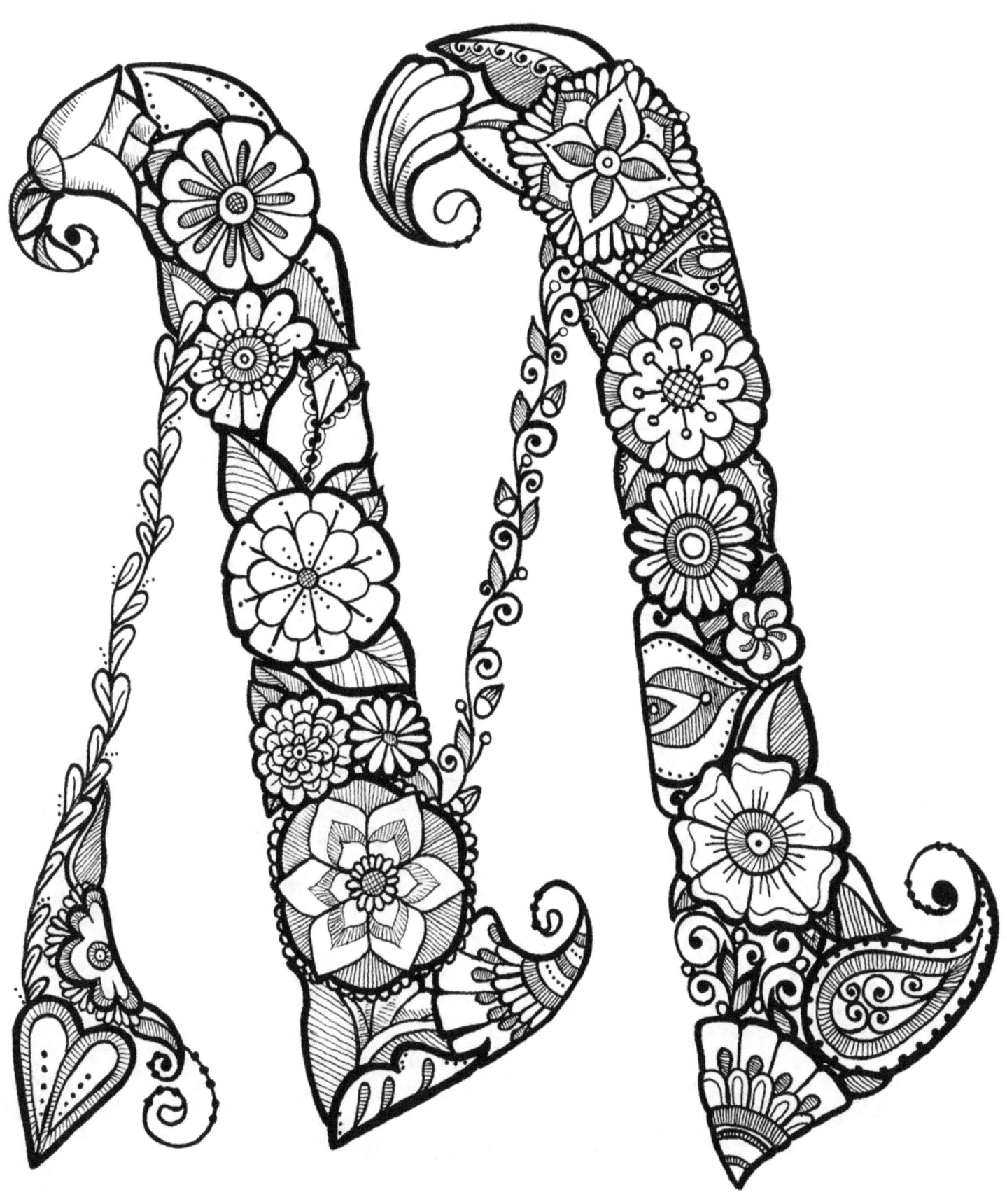

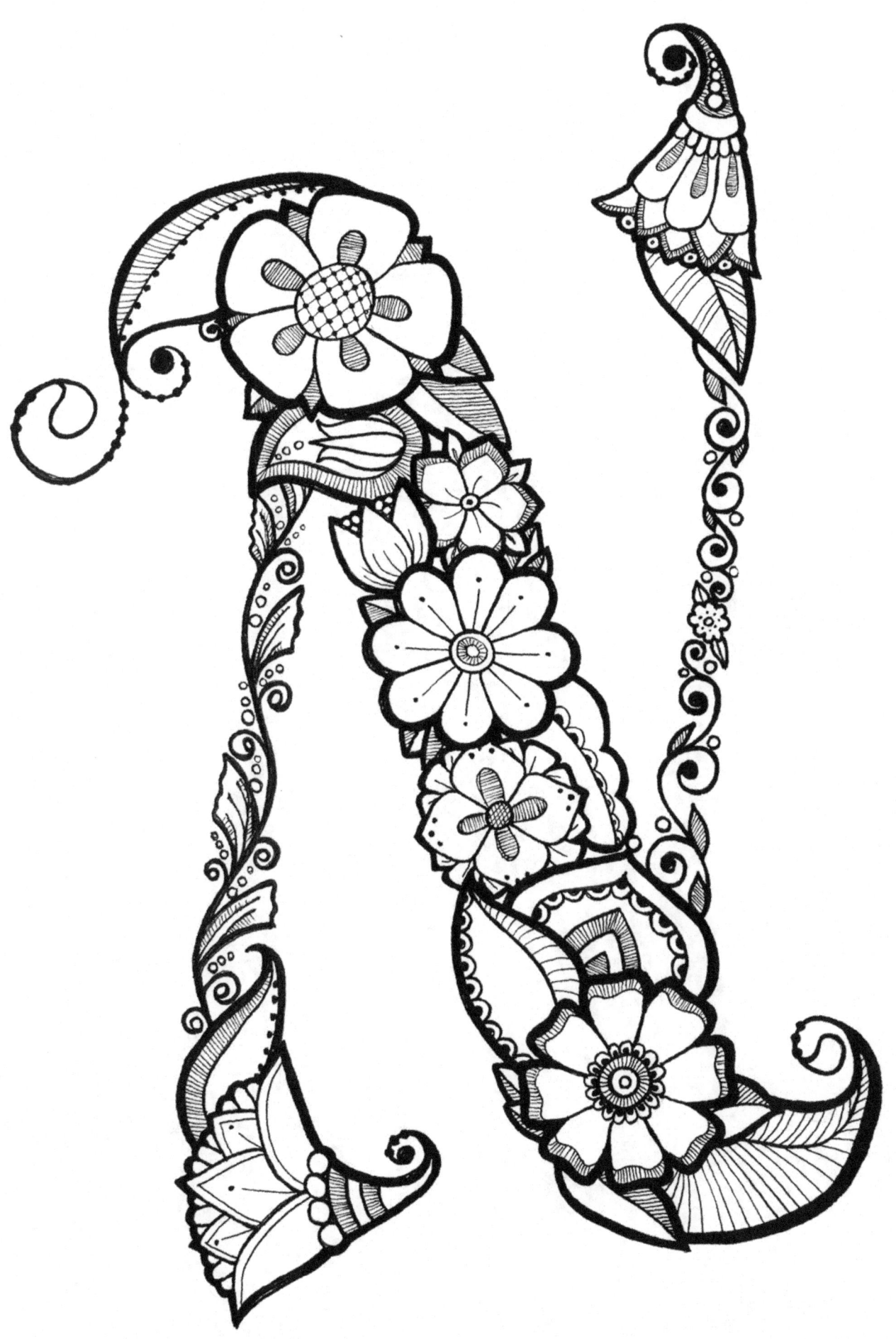

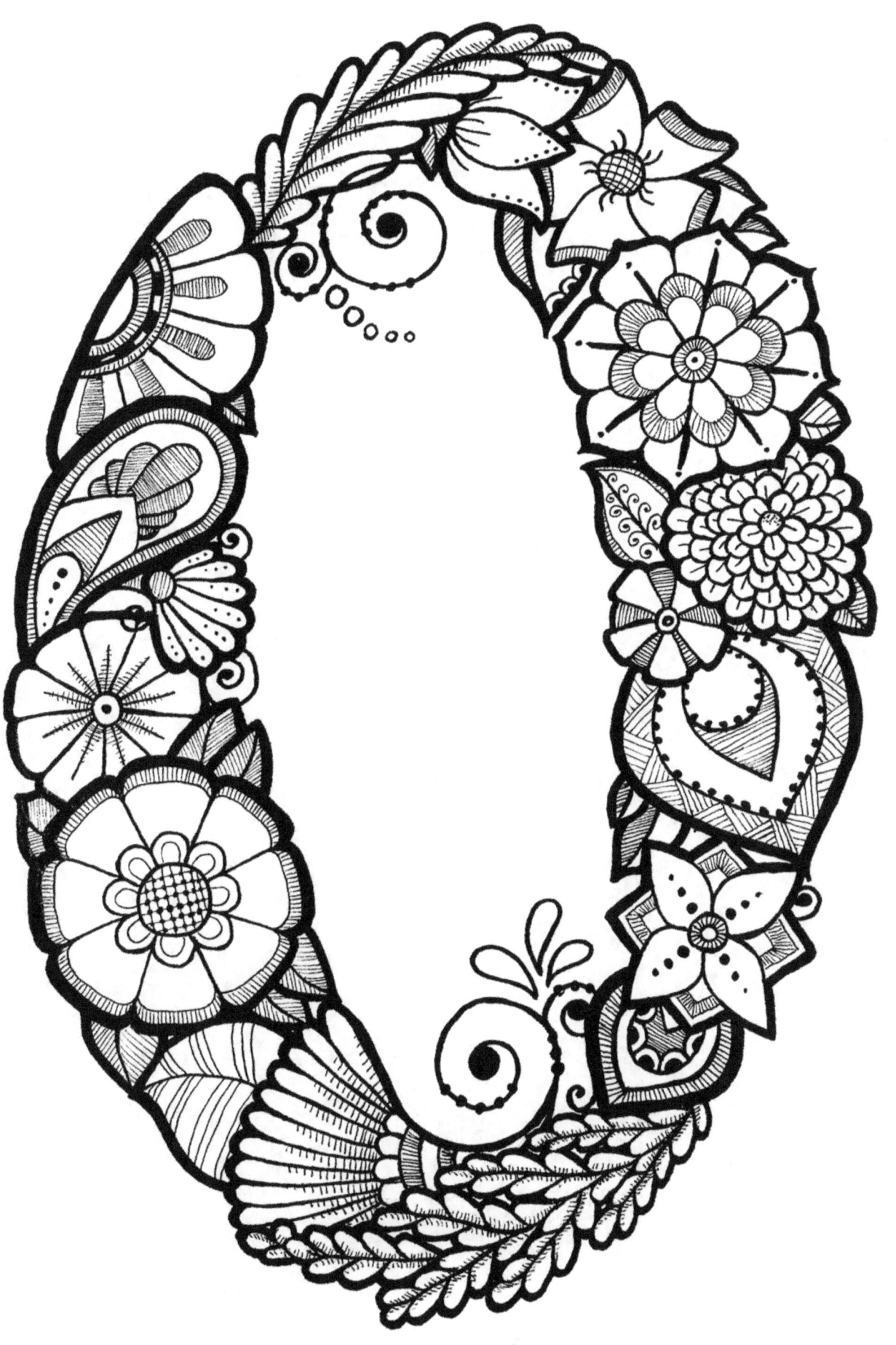

This Page Intentionally Left Blank

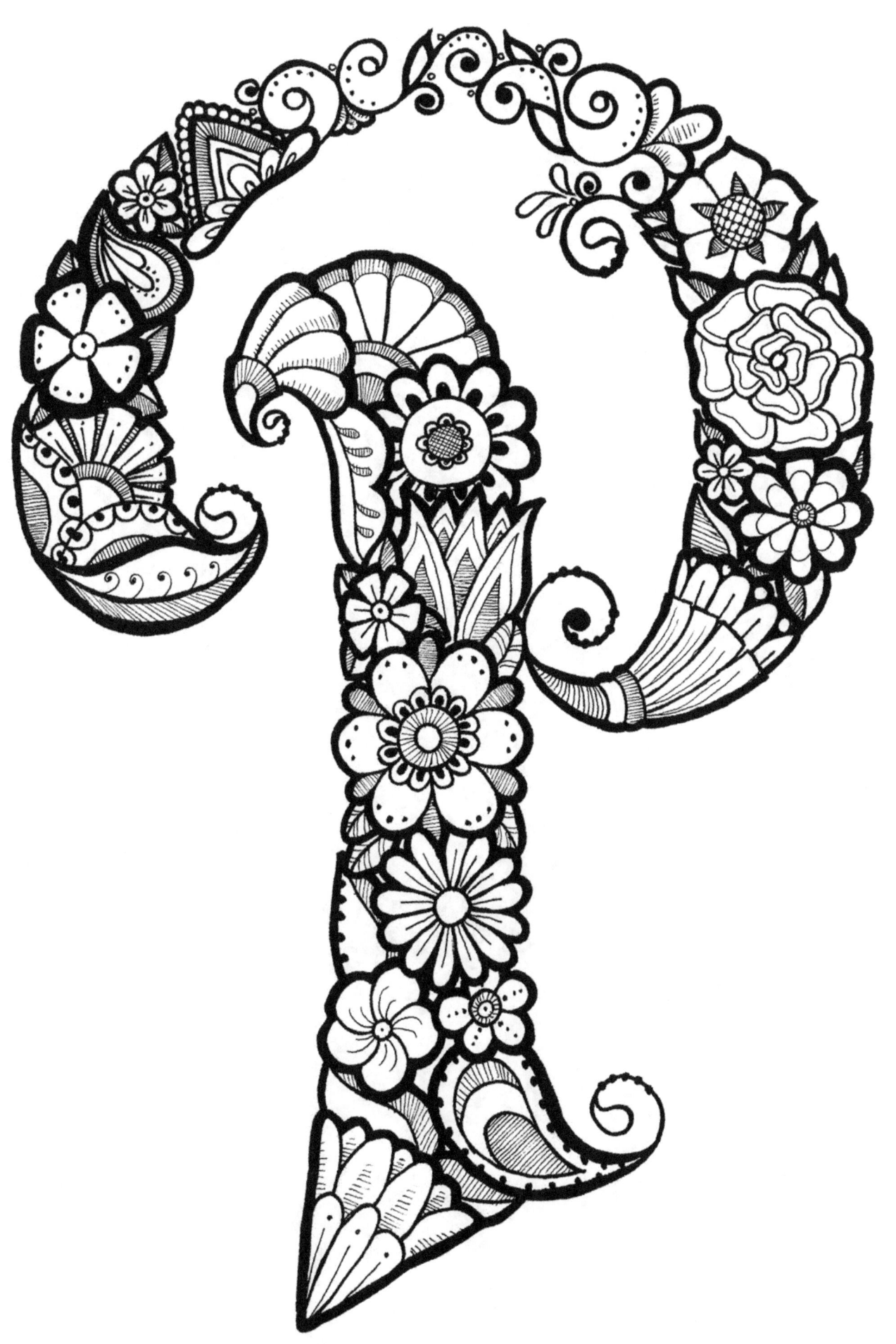

This Page Intentionally Left Blank

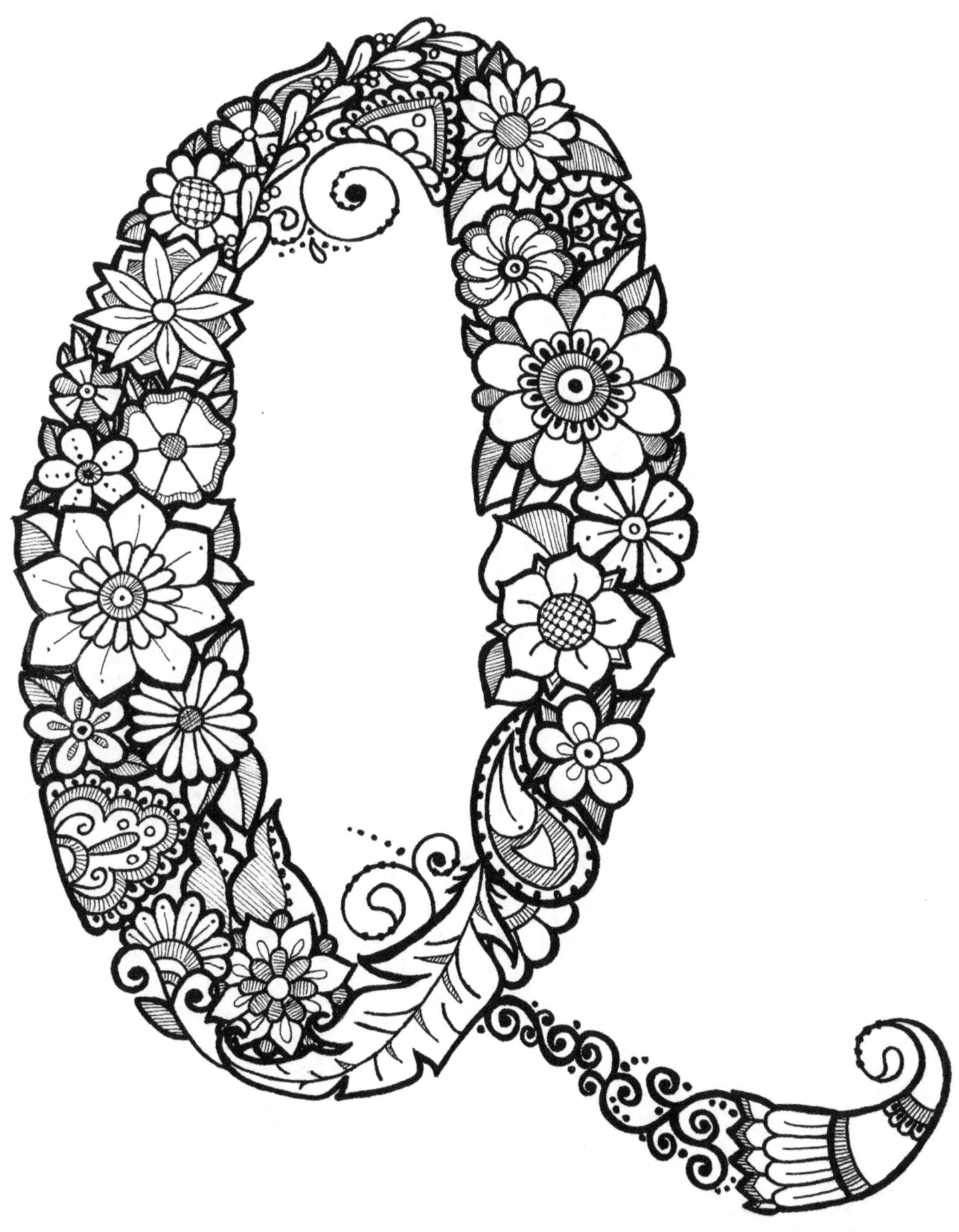

This Page Intentionally Left Blank

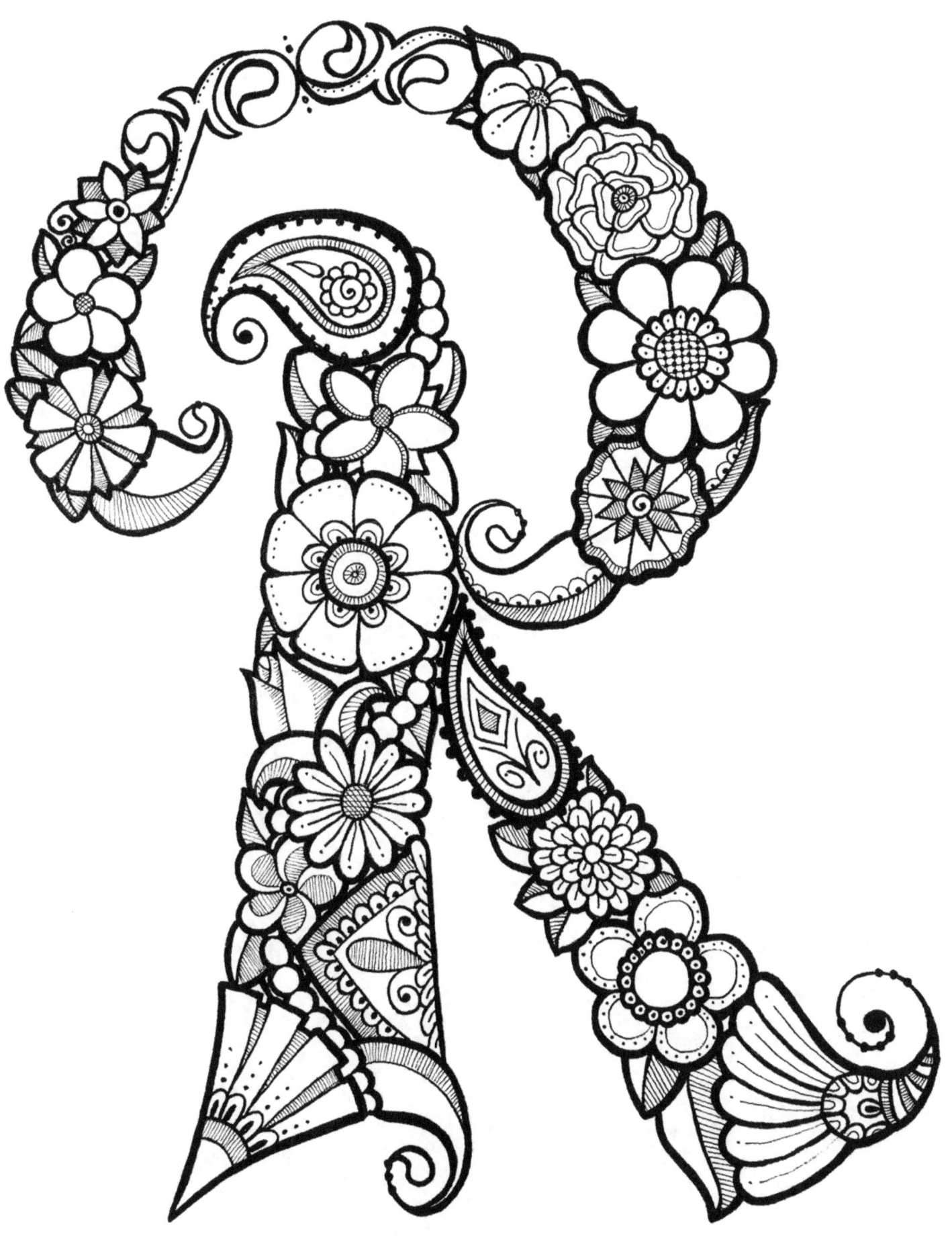

This Page Intentionally Left Blank

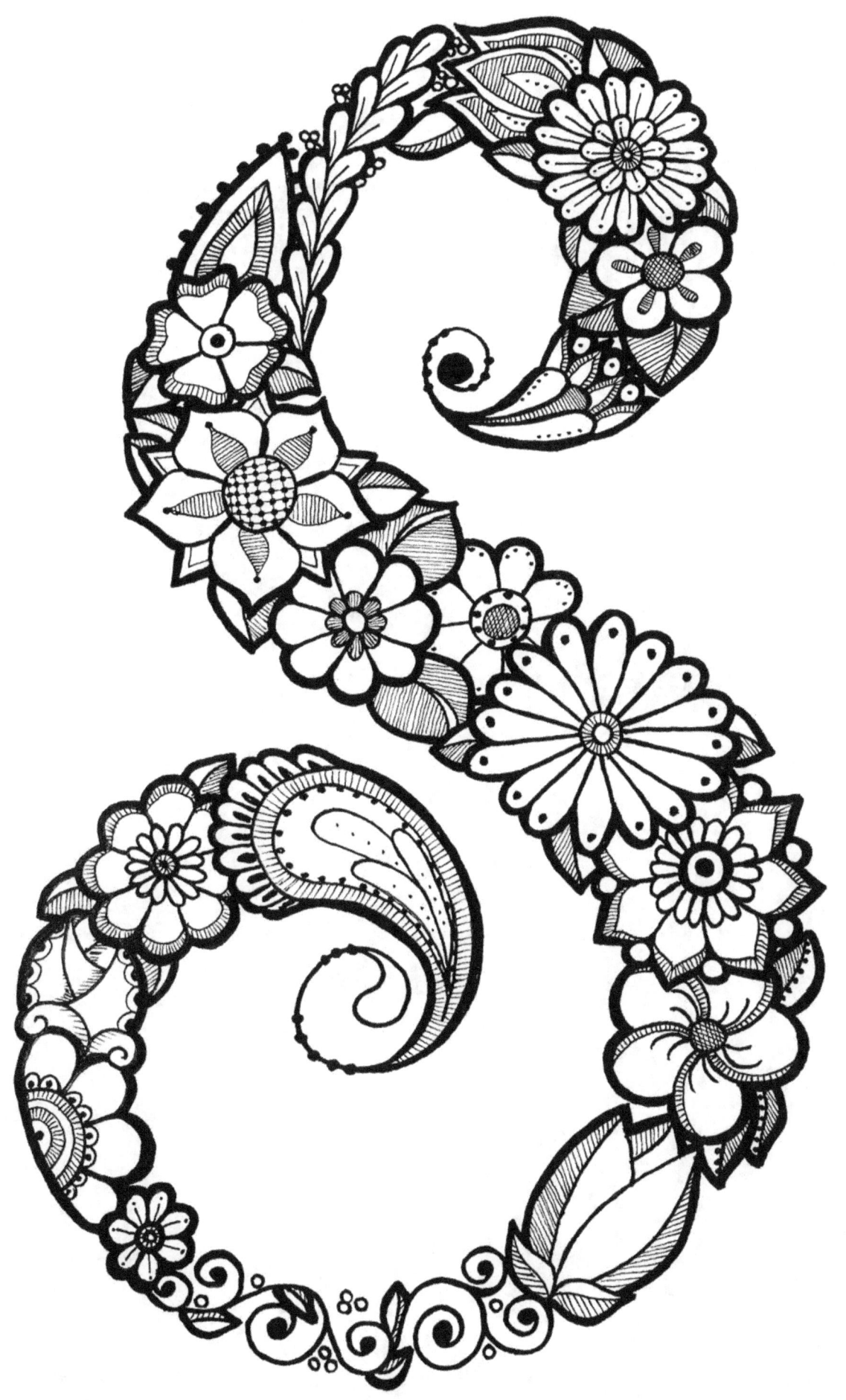

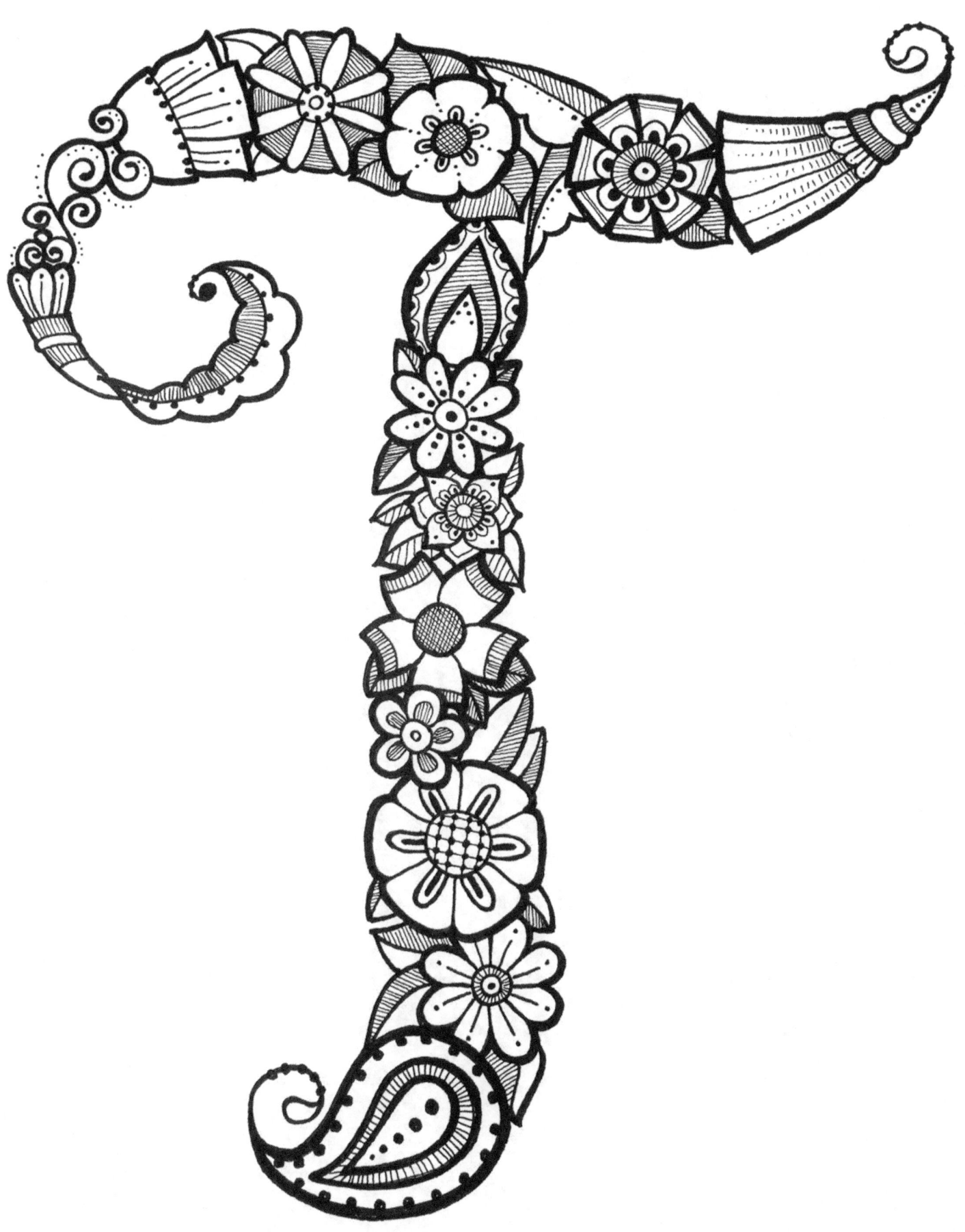

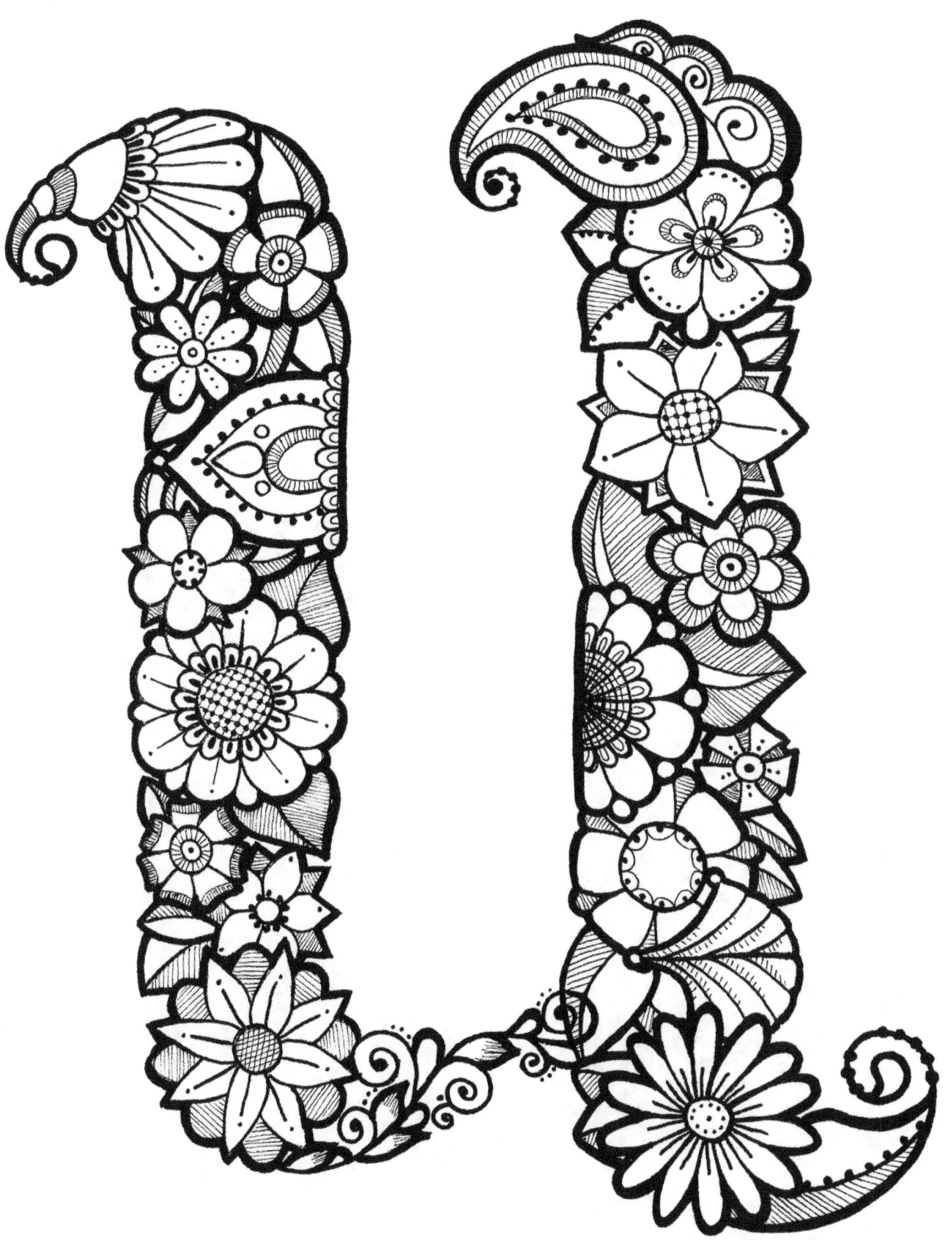

This Page Intentionally Left Blank

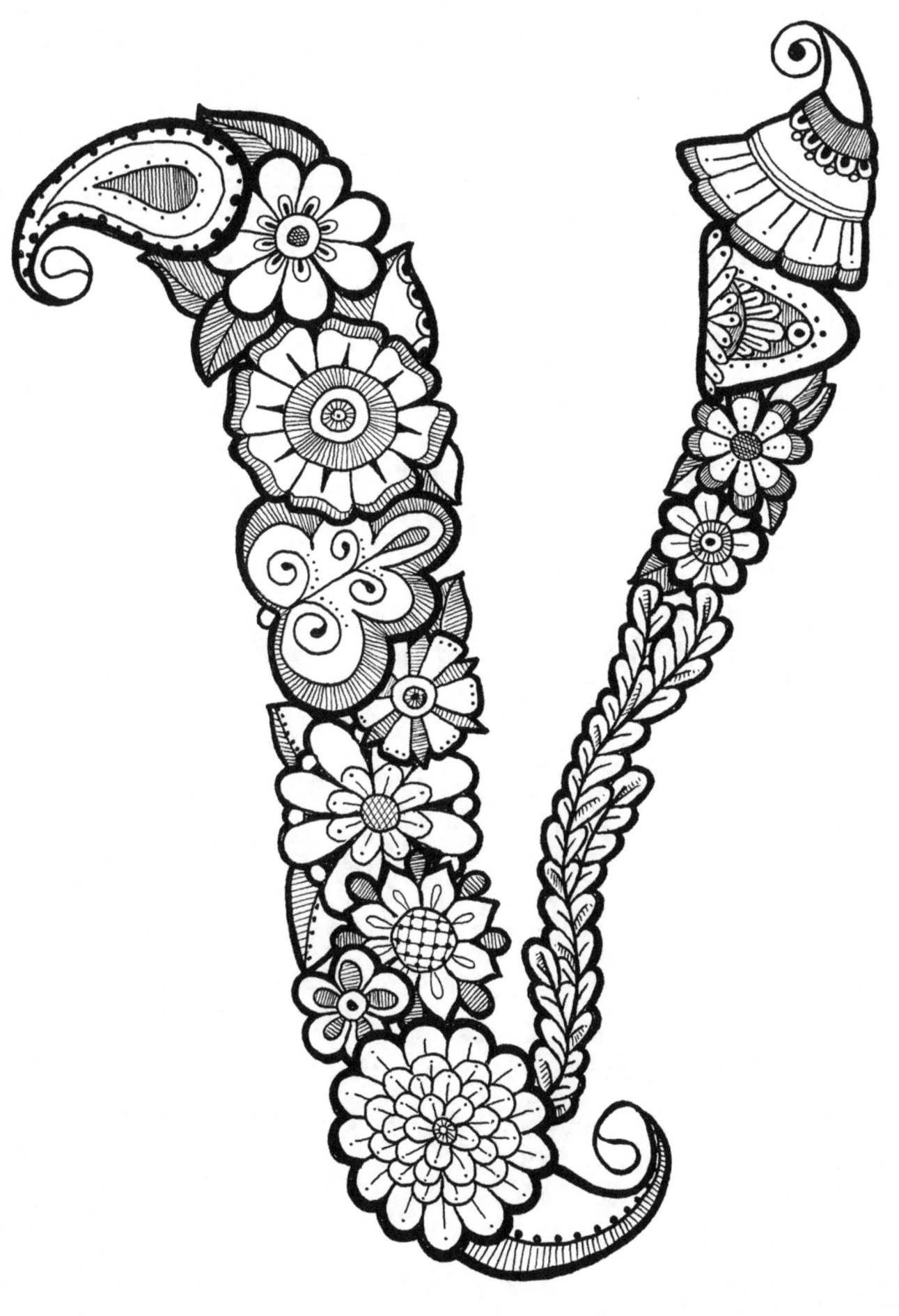

This Page Intentionally Left Blank

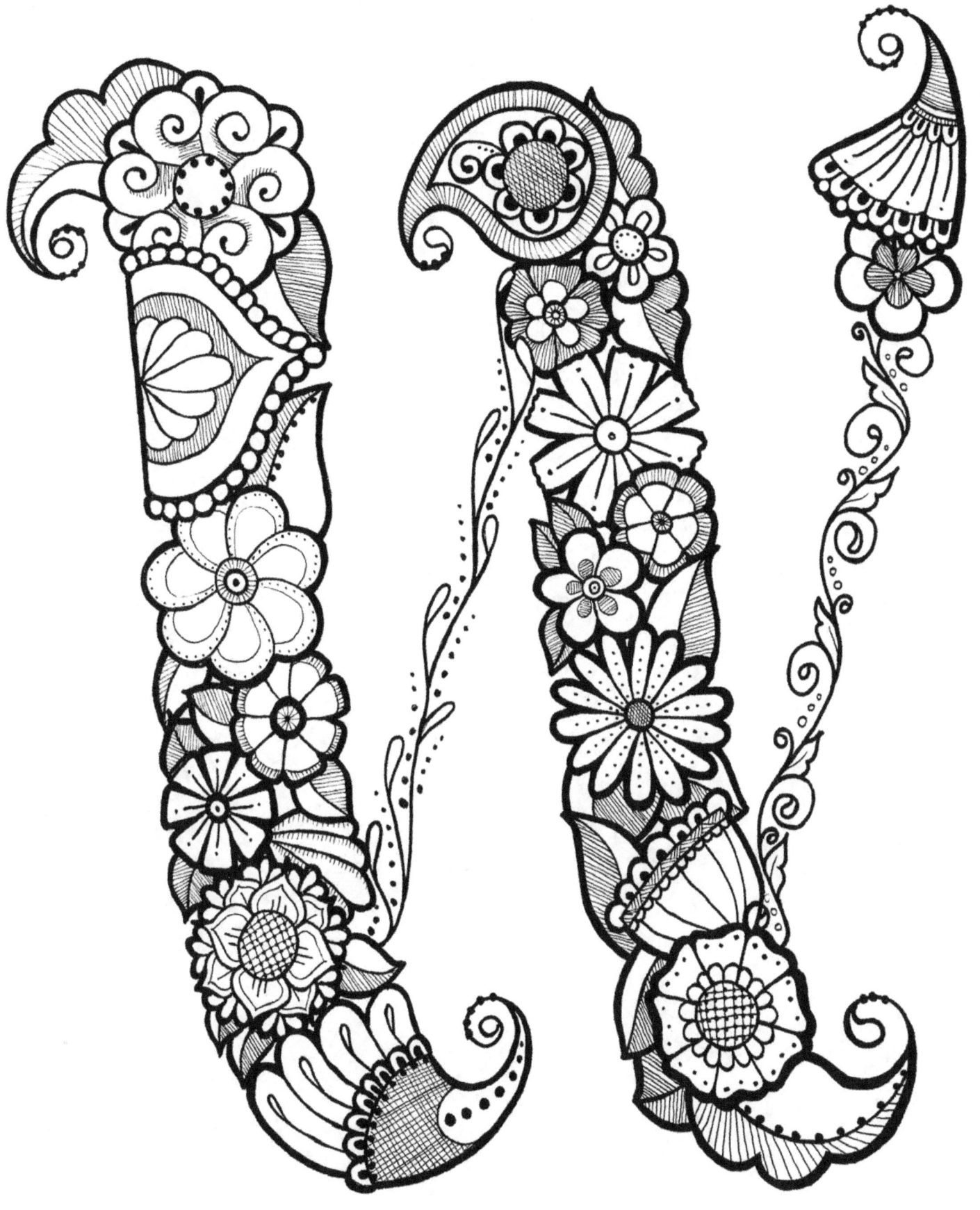

This Page Intentionally Left Blank

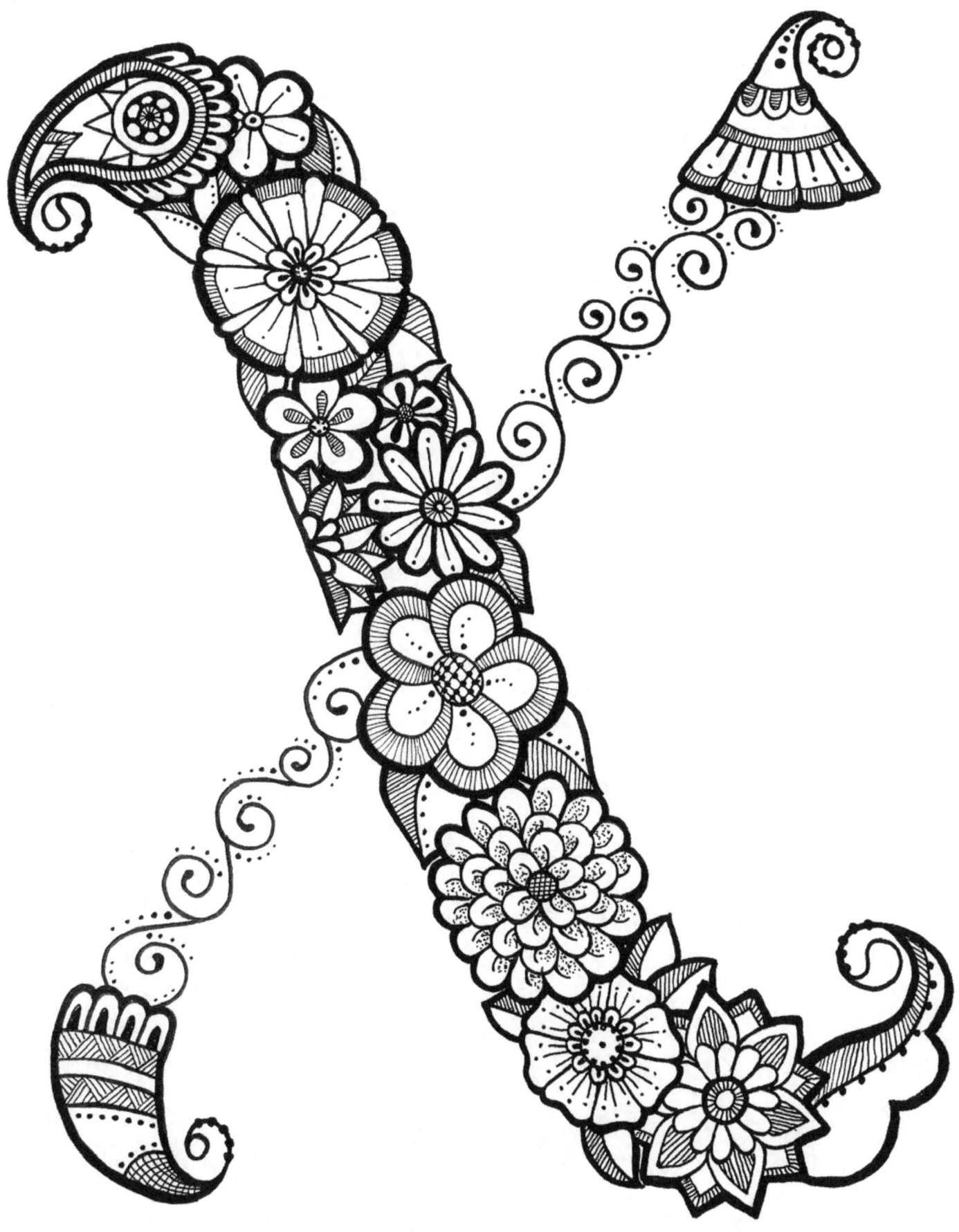

This Page Intentionally Left Blank

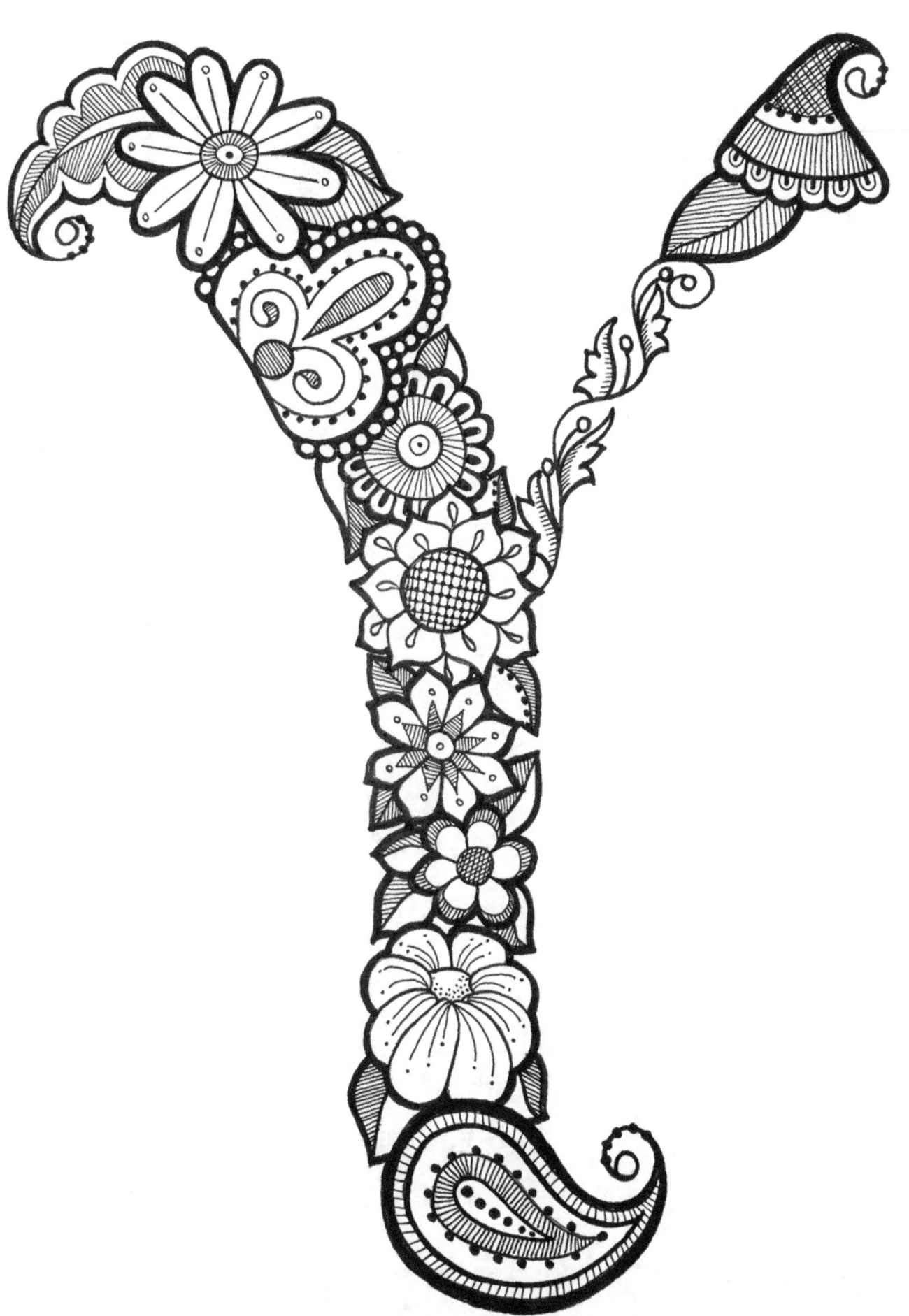

This Page Intentionally Left Blank

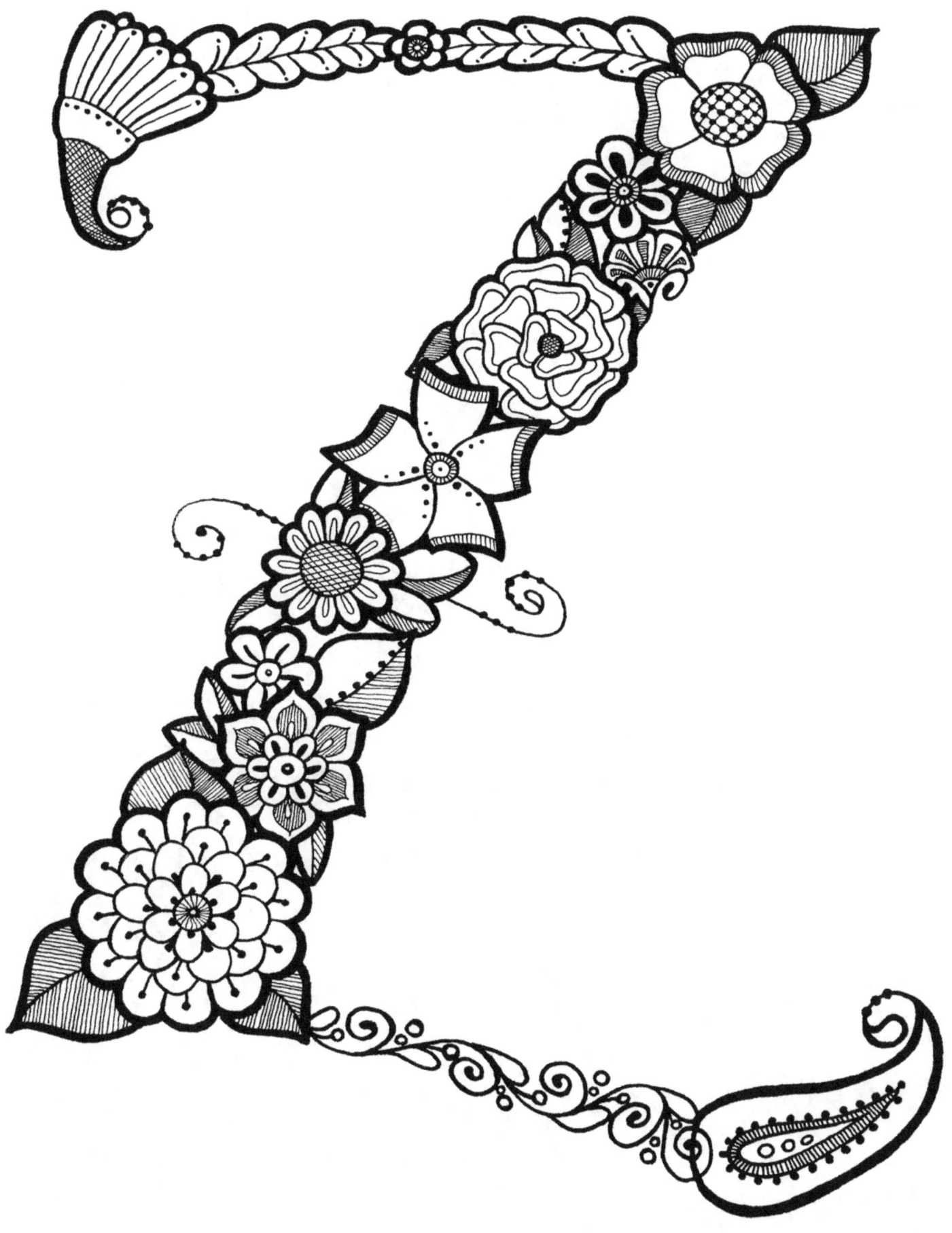

This Page Intentionally Left Blank

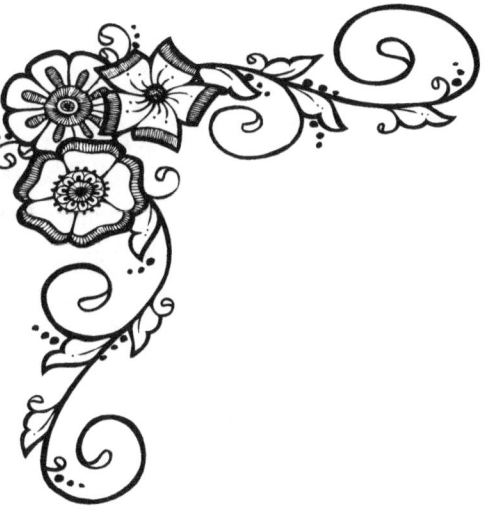
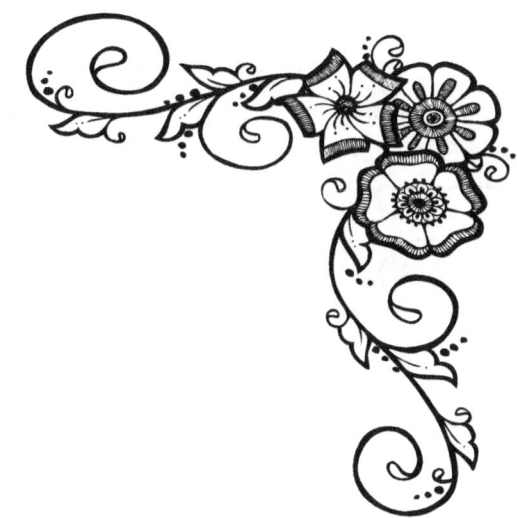

Published by Creative Spark Publishing

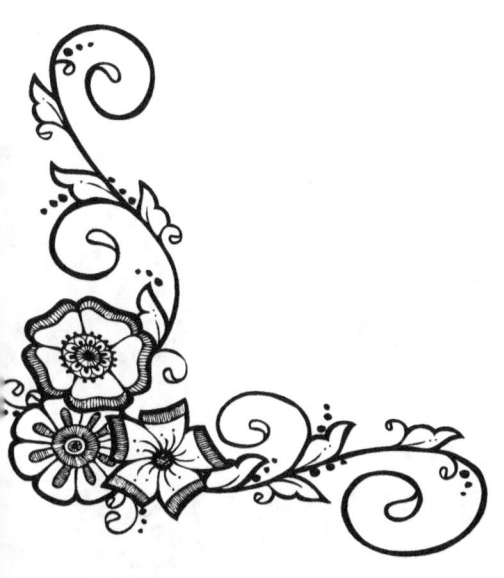

www.ingramcontent.com/pod-product-compliance
Lightning Source LLC
Chambersburg PA
CBHW080843170526
45158CB00009B/2616